PEARLS *of*
GRACE

31 DAY DEVOTIONAL

RASHANDA N. FOSTER

Limits of Liability and Disclaimer of Warranty

Cover Design: Studio 5 Agency www.studio5agency.com

Keen Vision Publishing, LLC
www.keen-vision.com

Printed in the United States of America
ISBN: 978-0-9992657-4-1

"A pearl is a beautiful thing that is produced by an injured life. It is the tear [that results] from the injury of the oyster. The treasure of our being in this world is also produced by an injured life. If we had not been wounded, if we had not been injured, then we will not produce the pearl."

-Stephen A Hoeller

Acknowledgements

Mom, thank you for being by my side through everything. You are more than a mother; you are my friend. I've watched you sacrifice so much for Reggie and me. Each day that I live, I want to make you proud and let you know that your sacrifices were not in vain. You are a true woman of God and the woman I hope to be. I honestly believe that I wouldn't be in the place I am today if it weren't for your love, prayers, and support. You encourage me, pour wisdom into me, and share the Word of God with me daily. Thank you for being my biggest cheerleader and prayer partner. You have pushed me for so many years to walk in boldness and share my truth. I appreciate you for all you've done to help bring my dream of being an author to reality. I love you dearly. Grandmom and Granddaddy, thank you for your love and support. You have been a constant source of wisdom and strength in my life. Your marriage of over 61 years and love you have for the family has been an example for me to follow. I love you both more than you will ever know.

Daddy Mike, you came into my life 19 years ago, and you've been a wonderful father to us and husband to my mother. You accepted me as if I was your blood daughter. You call me your princess, and you treat me as if I were one. I am so appreciative of your love for my mother and for being the example of the type of man I needed as a husband. Thank you for always encouraging and supporting me in the good times and the bad.

Corban, my precious little man boy. Since you entered this world, you have been my prized possession and greatest motivator. During some of the most difficult times in my life, you were the fuel I needed when I was running on fumes. The times I felt like throwing in the towel you were my reason not to give up. Thank you for holding me accountable for getting my writing done. You are my pride and joy. Thank you for giving me ideas for my business and things to include in my book. I'm so proud to be your mother. I love you more than you'll ever know.

Margaret Young, you are a woman of high strength. I thank you for accepting me as your daughter and not your step-daughter. You encouraged me to write my truth no matter what. Thank you for your sweet spirit, kind words, and encouragement.

Freda "Peaches," thank you for being more of a sister than a cousin. You have been with me through it all. You have encouraged me to not allow situations and people to discourage me from doing what God has called me to do. I appreciate and love you so much.

Yvette Torbert, thank you for being a great Woman of God. You are always encouraging and supporting my family and me. I appreciate you for accepting the challenge with me to complete my devotional in 30 days.

Carolita, my best friend for the past three decades. Thanks for being a true friend, encourager, sister, and supporter. I love you!

Maleeka Holloway, my writing coach extraordinaire, words can't express how grateful I am for you. Your encouragement, guidance, and expertise have been pivotal to me during this writing process.

Special thanks to Pastor T. C. Johnson, Apostle Eugene Florence, and Pastor Alzata Florence. Thank you all so much for your spiritual guidance. Your words of encouragement and inspiration through the preaching and teaching of the Word of God have been a blessing.

Finally, Tracey, you are truly a God send. I'm grateful to be your wife. You are an amazing husband and Man of God. Thank you for pushing me to walk in my purpose. You listen to my dreams, wipe away my tears, encourage me when I feel defeated, cover me in prayer, and love me wholeheartedly. You are the love of my life and my best friend. I can't imagine my life without you. Thank you for being the perfect husband

and an excellent father to our boys Tracey Jr., Treshaun, and Corban. I love you with everything in me.

About the Author

Rashanda Foster was born and raised in Eufaula, Alabama by a single mother with the help of her maternal grandparents. A graduate of Troy State University and Alabama A & M University, Rashanda earned her Master's Degree in counseling Psychology with a Concentration in Rehabilitation Counseling.

She resides in Madison, Alabama with her husband and sons. Rashanda is active in the Women's Ministry, Marriage Ministry, and the Music Ministry at St. Luke Christian Church of Huntsville, Alabama. She is a woman rooted and grounded in rich biblical tradition. She exemplifies the meaning of a Proverbs 31 woman. Rashanda has a heart for God and all special gift in encouraging, empowering, and supporting people especially women through sharing her testimony of God's grace.

Contents

Introduction

Several years ago, after going through a divorce, I was broken and dealt with internal issues that had not been addressed. Additionally, I had the task of adjusting to being a single mother. I sought God for His help like never before. I told God that I just wanted to be closer to Him, be at peace, and be able to raise my son. Little did I know, my gift of writing would begin shortly after those declarations. I had received two prophesies by total strangers, six years apart, that there was a ministry for women inside of me and there were books for me to write to encourage other broken women. These prophecies further confirmed my call to write books to help women who were dealing with issues from their past.

The Holy Spirit inspired this devotional, *Pearls of Grace.* I thought about how a strand of pearls represents elegance for most women. The making of a pearl is an extraordinary process. The pearl is unlike any other gem. Although beautiful, the irritation and pain to an oyster were necessary for its creation. The pearl is a symbol of perseverance because of how it's produced. I visualized each pearl on the necklace as an unpleasant experience I endured that made me better.

Like a pearl, we all have been affected in some way by external forces resulting in some uncomfortable situations, but we persevered. All my life experiences, the good, the bad, and the not so beautiful, played a role in the woman I am today. If you're reading this devotional, it is because you desire a closer walk with the Lord or you want something in this book to speak to your present situation. My heartfelt desire is that you will see that you are not alone in your situation. Like you, I am a woman who has been bruised by life, made bad choices, and desired a closer relationship with the Lord. Have you experienced life changing events that left you with wounds? Has the absence of your father left you looking for love in all the wrong places? Have you suffered sexual assault or physical abuse from someone you thought loved you? Have the past hurts affected your self- worth? Many times, as women, we suffer in silence. We put on a good face for everyone, but inside we are slowly dying. Pearls of Grace shares scriptures that speak to pieces of my testimony and will address these issues. It is designed to encourage, empower, and uplift women. Through my trials and triumphs, I hope that your lives will be touched. Hopefully, by reading all 31 days, you will receive joy, healing, deliverance, peace, the Love of God, and understanding. In each devotional, you can expect to learn how I was able to overcome some of the most difficult times and how I used scripture to encourage me along life's journey.

Before we begin....

- ❖ List the difficult moments you've endured along your life journey.

_____

_____

_____

_____

_____

_____

_____

_____

_____

_____

_____

Pearls of Grace

Pearl One

Priceless Pearls

"Again, the Kingdom of Heaven is like a merchant on the lookout for choice pearls. When he discovered a pearl of great value, he sold everything he owned and bought it!"

Matthew 13:45-46 (NLT)

As a young girl, pearls were never appealing to me. I always associated pearls with little old ladies, because they were the only people I saw wearing them. Once, I went away to college and pledged Alpha Kappa Alpha Sorority, Incorporated, my opinion of pearls quickly changed. I began to see pearls through different lenses. Therefore, I began to wear them and realized that pearls were elegant and made every outfit look good.

An authentic set of pearls is expensive because they are precious. The pearl represents Jesus Christ and the salvation He offers to each of us. In the parable (Matthew 13), Jesus likened the merchant finding precious pearls to us finding the Kingdom of Heaven. We could never pay for salvation; the Kingdom of Heaven is invaluable. Once we receive salvation, like the merchant in the parable, we should be willing to give up everything to keep it. We often don't seek

God until we've grown tired of the unnecessary searching in relationships, alcohol and drugs, and material things. However, we must understand that Jesus Christ does something no person or thing can do for us. He fulfills our greatest hopes, satisfies our needs, calms our fears, heals our hearts, and cleans us and makes us whole before the Father.

It wasn't until I became older that the value of pearls became real to me. I believe that going through and enduring the trials and tests of life embodies grace thus making our witness invaluable to the Kingdom of God. It's hard to be a witness when you haven't gone through any trying times. When we are blinded by our mediocre surroundings and limited thinking, we miss the inherent value of Jesus Christ, the precious gift of salvation in our lives, and the grace given to us during our most difficult times. I gained a pearl through every experience God gave me the grace to get through.

Today, I wear my pearls proudly because I know their worth. I also know that anything precious to God will be tested for authenticity.

REFLECTIONS

Are you devaluing your pearls because of what it took to get them?

_____

_____

_____

_____

_____

_____

_____

_____

_____

_____

_____

Do Not Disturb

You will keep in perfect peace all who trust in you, all whose thoughts are fixed on you!

Isaiah 26:3 (NLT)

Have you ever embarked on a new situation such as a job or relationship and it seemed to be a struggle from the very start? You're not at peace in the situation and no matter how you try to fix it, the situation continues to get worse. Many times, we encounter these struggles because we failed to consult with God before we entered the situation in the first place. Thus, the constant struggle is because we are living out of the will of God. Isaiah 26: 3 simply tells us that if we keep our thoughts on God and trust in Him to guide us, He will keep us in perfect peace.

One morning while getting ready for work, I started praising God for a peaceful sleep. You see, it had not been that long ago when I prayed for a good night's sleep. For years, I was unable to get a full night's rest. Each morning, I would wake up exhausted and go through my days in a fog. I can recall taking countless sleep aids and sleeping pills to sleep to no avail. God showed me that at that time, I was trying to do things on my own with no regard to Him. When you're in His will, He can and will give you peace in the midst of your issues, problems, and troubles. I am so thankful that I surrendered my will to God and let Him take the lead in the dance of my life.

My life is in no way perfect and I don't have it all together, but I am so thankful to God for the peace I have in my home, mind, and spirit despite the troubles that may arise. I am learning to not only trust God with the big decisions but with the small ones as well. Reading His word and praying daily helps me keep my mind on Him. Today, I don't take a peaceful night's sleep or my peace of mind for granted! When you're not in God's will, it can disturb every area of your life. When you let go of those things that are disturbing your peace, that's when you begin to live!

You don't have stress or worry about whether you are where you need to be or if you have made the right decision. God says that if you keep your mind on Him and trust in His will for your life, He will keep you in perfect peace.

REFLECTIONS

- ❖ What is disturbing your peace, stifling your progress, or keeping you out of the will of God?

- ❖ Do you commune with God daily for guidance and peace?

Heavy Load

For our light affliction, which is but for a moment, works
for us a far more exceeding and eternal weight of glory.

II Corinthians 4:17 (NLT)

There was a time in my life when I felt like a failure. I was ashamed, depressed, and overwhelmed with my plight. The generational curses I vowed to break took over my life for the world to see and judge. I never thought I'd be divorced and a single mom. On one of those difficult days, these words from my mother encouraged and inspired me. She said, "Rashanda, hold your head up. How you get through this test determines how you come out of it. You can choose to be a victim or a victor."

I couldn't allow my circumstances to affect the way I look, treated others, or my outlook on life. I believe that everything we go through serves a divine purpose. We all will have our loads to carry. I know now that God didn't put more on me than I could bear. When my spirit tries to get weak, I remind myself that my present circumstances are just temporary.

Are you feeling overwhelmed with life? Does it weigh you down mentally and physically? Please understand that sulking, complaining, and crying about it is only making it worse. Pick yourself up and see your situation through the eyes of Jesus Christ. Jesus carried a far greater load. Your situation to Him is nothing. He paid the ultimate price for the both of us, and He was without sin or fault. Although Jesus knew he was carrying out the will of The Father, he pressed His way carrying the weight of our sins on his back.

If I had not experienced tough times, I wouldn't have been moved to share with others. Just as God did with Jesus, He is going to get the glory out of your situation too. C. S. Lewis said it best, "It's not the load that breaks you, it's how you carry it." I encourage you to carry your weight with grace. What you're going through right now is not just for you, but for others who will be strengthened and blessed by your experience and testimony.

REFLECTIONS

What are you willing to do to rid yourself of the load you're carrying?

Let It Go

Finally, all of you should be of one mind. Sympathize with each other. Love each other as brothers and sisters. Be tenderhearted, and keep a humble attitude. Don't repay evil for evil. Don't retaliate with insults when people insult you. Instead, pay them back with a blessing. That is what God has called you to do, and he will grant you his blessing.

I Peter 3:8-9 (NLT)

It's so easy to retaliate when you've been done wrong, but what does it prove? Being able to love and pray for those who hurt us is an incredible strength. Jesus Christ provides the greatest example of strength in the midst of adversity. The fact that He was wrongly accused, mocked, beaten, and hung on the cross just to die for us renders me speechless. What we go through in life just doesn't compare to all the Savior endured.

Peter saw firsthand how Jesus suffered unjustly at the hands of his enemies without retaliation. I imagine that witnessing such courage and restraint moved Peter to speak to us on how we should conduct ourselves when we're attacked by the adversary. We all know right from wrong but how many of us can say that our carnal mind doesn't initially go into attack mode when we've been hurt or offended by someone?

Perhaps you are holding on to an offense and don't know how to let it go. One of the secrets to keeping the peace in any relationship is not to allow hard feelings, resentment, or hostility to linger! It's okay to calm down, pray, and think about your approach, but remember the saying "study long you study wrong." As Christians, we should be willing to pray for our brothers and sisters with the same conviction Jesus did. Make it your mission to let go of the resentment and anger and be the bigger person in every situation regardless of how you feel.

REFLECTIONS

Is it difficult for you to let go of an offense?

_____

_____

_____

_____

_____

_____

_____

_____

_____

_____

_____

_____

_____

Pearl Five

Broken but Useful

He heals the brokenhearted and binds up their wounds.

Psalms 147:3 (NIV)

While coloring with my son Corban, my pink crayon broke. He immediately said, "Ahh, Mommy, your crayon is broken. I have to throw it away because I can't use it anymore!" I thought this was such a teachable moment. I explained to my then four-year-old that just because it's broken doesn't mean it can't be used again. I further explained how that same broken crayon still colors the same as it did when it was whole. Although the crayon broke, it still served a purpose.

If you read through your Bible, you will see that God didn't use many people who lived perfect lives. God used broken people like Saul, a murderer; Rahab, the prostitute; Samson, the womanizer; and Noah, a drunk. God mends us when we're broken, hurting, and think we are beyond repair. We can't throw people and things away because they're broken. God can use our brokenness for His glory if we allow him to. I'm a witness to that!

Perhaps you feel like you've made a mess of things and God won't come to your rescue. There is nothing we can do that will disqualify us from being used by God. There's a purpose for your pain. Often, brokenness will come before the blessing.

REFLECTIONS

Have life's circumstances left you feeling useless to God?

_____

_____

_____

_____

_____

_____

_____

_____

_____

_____

_____

_____

Pearl Six

Giant Slayer

We use God's mighty weapons, not worldly weapons to knock down strongholds of human reasoning and destroy false arguments.

2 Corinthians 10:4 (NLT)

If you haven't heard the popular internet term "slay," you've been living under a rock. The slang term *slay* means to dominate something or to own it. Many use *slay* to describe the appearance of something such as a person's hair, makeup, or attire. After hearing this word so much, I began to ask myself, "What would happen if we focused more on slaying the enemy who seeks to destroy us?"

Before I proceed, I'm in total agreement that we should always look our best and present our best to the world. However, what's the point of looking good but spiritually ineffective? God has given us the authority to tear down barriers designed to work against God's truths. That means our looks alone can't and won't destroy the works of the enemy. The supernatural power that works within us will if we choose to use it. We have the authority to slay in the spirit anything that attempts to disrupt our peace of mind, family, finances, happiness, and health.

The enemy is not afraid of a woman that's well dressed with a made-up face; he's afraid of a woman who boldly wears the full armor of God and uses it daily. We are giant slayers!

REFLECTIONS

Are you using your God given power to slay the enemy and his attacks?

_____

_____

_____

_____

_____

_____

_____

_____

_____

_____

_____

_____

Pearl Seven

The Thirst Is Real

Jesus replied "But those who drink the water I give will never be thirsty again. It becomes a fresh, bubbling spring within them, giving them eternal life."

John 4: 14 (NLT)

The story of the Samaritan woman at the well is a great example of deliverance and grace. It is important to understand that water in its natural state is satisfying and necessary for human life and vegetation. People, animals, and plants need the nourishment from water to live. Therefore, water is life. However, in this passage, water represented the eternal life that only God can give. Jesus was thirsty for water but took the time to talk with this woman who was an outcast and an immoral woman. He was acutely aware of her sins and her enormous spiritual thirst. He also knew she was making a mess of her life because she was looking for love in all the wrong places.

I can relate to the Samaritan woman. I briefly dated after my divorce but wasn't satisfied. I felt like there was something more. I ended a five-month dating relationship with a good man because I felt unfulfilled. I wanted to better my relationship with God, and that relationship would hinder me from doing that. I realized early on that I needed a man of God in my life who is able and willing to cover me in prayer. Unfortunately, he wasn't that man. I recall telling my mother my decision to end the relationship. I told her that I'd be satisfied with raising my son and living for the Lord. I also said that if I decide to marry again, God would have to give me every sign in the beginning that he is the man for me. I rededicated my life to Christ that day and engulfed myself in the word and ministry at my church.

This meeting at the well transformed the life of this woman. Jesus explained to her that her needs would only be fulfilled by finding and making God the most vital relationship in her life. Little did I know, my thirst for something more was a closer relationship with God. The more I sought Him, the more my life began to change for the better. Just like the woman at the well, to quench this thirst, we should ask God to do it. He provides a never-ending supply of whatever we need throughout our relationship with him. I know from experience that we can have whatever we desire if we just ask. Having your needs met by Jesus makes all the difference.

REFLECTIONS

❖ Are you dying of spiritual thirst?

❖ Do you find yourself seeking acceptance and love from men but left thirsting for something more?

Pearls of Grace

Pearl Eight

Pain Is Gain

It was good for me to be afflicted so that I might learn your decrees.

Psalms 119:71 (NIV)

Remember your Mom telling you as a toddler not to touch something that was hot? You didn't understand what she meant until you felt it and got burned! The injury (pain) taught you a valuable lesson. The next time, you knew the consequence of doing the opposite of what you're told. Pain is sometimes a result of not following instructions. We carry this into our adulthood as well. Sometimes, we get out of the will (relationships, jobs, finances, etc.) of God because we fail to do things his way. The consequence is pain that can not only affect us but those around us as well.

Pain does not feel good at the time but often proves to be beneficial. You often hear personal trainers say, "If it's not hurting, it's not working." You never know how strong you are until you've been challenged. As an adult, I have made several bad decisions in relationships and finances. Many times, I failed to seek God and set aside my spiritual beliefs for the things that I wanted. Those bad decisions left me feeling ashamed, lost, and helpless. However, all those situations resulted in me crying out to the Lord for help. Therefore, the pain increased my prayer life and strengthened my relationship with The Lord.

Pain is inevitable. The presence of pain, especially after making a wrong decision, can be devastating. However, isn't it a blessing to know that the pain can make you better if you don't let it paralyze you? Pain often forces us to change because we will likely think about the consequences and choose another course of action when encountering certain situations in the future. The struggle you are experiencing today is equipping you with the strength you'll need for tomorrow. In other words, the pain you feel today is empowering you for the endurance you will need in the future. Just remember your suffering is not in vain, there's a lesson! It was for your good!

REFLECTIONS

Are you letting the pain of what happened make you bitter or better?

_____

_____

_____

_____

_____

_____

_____

_____

_____

_____

_____

Pearl Nine

Unbothered

Be anxious for nothing, but in everything by prayer and supplication, with thanksgiving, let your requests be made known to God: and the peace of God, which surpasses all understanding, will guard your hearts and minds through Christ Jesus.

Philippians 4:6-7 (NLT)

This passage provides a clear picture of what we should do. God tells us NOT to worry about anything! That includes EVERYTHING....Yes, those bills, your life, children, job, health, and even the things you haven't thought of yet. This Bible verse doesn't promise that all your prayer requests will be answered. It says that when you're facing difficult situations, you will pray about them rather than worry.

I can recall when I was faced with depression after having a hysterectomy. I just knew that wasn't a part of my life plan. I had just gotten remarried to the man of my dreams three months prior. I wanted to have another child and be able to share that experience with my husband. It was devastating. I remember long days of crying, silence, and feeling like no one understood. It was as if I forgot for a moment that I was a woman of faith. I remember crying out to God and asking Him to give me peace of my mind and spirit so I could move on with my life. I thanked Him for giving me Corban, the one son I birthed. I asked God to forgive me for failing to recognize how blessed I was to already be a mother and bonus mother to my husband's sons. It wasn't until I took this scripture to heart and was completely honest with myself that I received what I had prayed for, peace.

Perhaps you are dealing with anxiety and depression that is causing sleepless nights. These feelings are robbing you of the peaceful life God desires for you. God is a burden lifter. Pray and ask God for what you want and see how He frees your mind, body, and spirit.

REFLECTIONS

What is disturbing your peace?

Pearls of Grace

Pearl Ten

Stay Holy

For the Scriptures say, "You must be holy because I am holy.

I Peter 1:16 (NLT)

One day, on my drive home from work, "Be Ye Holy, for I Am Holy" dropped in my spirit. I immediately thought about my growth in the Lord and the conversation I had that morning with my best friend, Carolita. We were praising God for keeping us when He was the furthest thing from our minds. As teenagers, we both did some things that we aren't proud of, but we rejoice now because we are both saved and living for the Lord.

I also thought about how my mother would call me when I was in college. Before hanging up, she would tell me to remain holy or keep it holy. I would either roll my eyes and rush her off the phone before I received a sermon, or laugh with my sorority sister, Cheryl, about it. Little did I know, my mother was dropping a nugget in my spirit so that when I went out or was doing things that I shouldn't be, *stay holy* would influence my decisions. Even though it didn't always deter me from participating in activities that weren't exactly "holy," it was always in the back of my mind.

Being holy is not a suggestion, it's a command from God. God wants us to be set apart. Holiness is a process that will not happen overnight. It only comes with trying, failing, and constant learning to live a life that's different from the world's standard. When we are holy, our primary focus is to live a life that's pleasing to God. Being holy is having a different set of priorities which are often exhibited through our actions.

I wondered why being in certain environments, doing certain things, and being around certain people didn't feel right to me. I just felt out of place. I understand that I was simply uncomfortable because I was in unholy places doing unholy things. My mother was giving me scripture to feed my soul and to remind me of how I needed to represent myself. I'm thankful that my mother planted those seeds in my mind early on. I'm even more grateful to God for his unfailing love.

REFLECTIONS

Are you living a life that's set apart? Are you Holy doing unholy things?

_____

_____

_____

_____

_____

_____

_____

_____

_____

_____

_____

_____

Pearl Eleven

Suddenly

And suddenly there was a great earthquake, so that the foundations of the prison were shaken: and immediately all the doors were opened, and every one's bands were loose.

Acts 16:26 (NLT)

After suffering heart problems because of severe stress from my job as a school counselor, it was recommended that I quit my job or die. After hearing this, I felt my life was having an earthquake. My husband assured me that we would be okay with one income, but we'd have to make some sacrifices. I turned in my resignation and left my career as a school counselor. The months ahead were very challenging for me because I was shaken to the core. It became a financial struggle for my household, but my husband never once complained.

After going back to the cardiologist for a check-up, he asked what had I done differently. My heart tests revealed there were no problems with my heart. I told him I quit my job. The doctor said, "You should've done that a long time ago." He stated that he wouldn't need to see me anymore and my heart was back to normal. I immediately started looking for jobs outside of the school system, but I landed flat on my face. I took a contract position doing group counseling with an agency that I'd worked for years ago. While thankful for the opportunity, the pay was meager. Despite the pay, I remained faithful. My husband and I praised God daily, prayed diligently, sowed into lives of others, and served faithfully in our church ministry.

In January 2015, during a late-night talk with my husband about the future and his retirement from the Army, we decided we'd have to leave the Eufaula area for better employment opportunities. We prayed and went to bed. The next morning, I went online to look for jobs in the Huntsville area. I applied for one position that required me to have military experience or be a military spouse. I received a call that same day from a recruiter for a pre-screening interview. Two days later, I was offered a job as a Government Contractor that included a salary that exceeded my expectations. Of course, I accepted.

This unexpected blessing blew my mind because I'd never experienced anything like this before. The shaking I experienced in my life was necessary. God honored our sincere prayers and faithfulness. He sustained us, and we didn't suffer any loss. Maybe you're in the middle of a prison moment in your life. We serve the same God that Paul and Silas were praying to and praising. I encourage you to continue giving God praise, keep the faith and believe that your break through is on the way. God has not forgotten about you; He is going to come to your rescue. He is working behind the scenes and strategically placing the right people and opportunities in your path to bless you.

REFLECTIONS

❖ Have you ever felt like you were a prisoner of life?

❖ What area in your life do you need a "sudden" blessing from God?

_____

_____

_____

_____

_____

_____

_____

_____

_____

_____

Rashanda Foster

Pearl Twelve

Shine

Let your light so shine before men, that they may see your good works, and glorify your Father which is in heaven.

Matthew 5:16 (KJV)

We all appreciate praise for what we do. Many people are driven by praise and recognition. Some wouldn't do good works if weren't for the gratification of praise it provides. I believe that is the reason that Jesus didn't just command that we do good works for the world to see, but that He gets the glory. Jesus always gave his Father credit or directed attention to his Father when being praised for his good works.

At nine-years-old, my son Corban is a stellar athlete, and I'm not saying that because he's my son. A few months after moving to a new city, we signed him up for a youth football team. He asked the coach if he could be a quarterback and the coach was kind enough to give him a chance. My husband and I were nervous because of his lack of experience. However, his first game calmed those fears instantly because he scored five touchdowns. We were so proud of him. He received praise from everyone, and it quickly went to his head.

It is so easy for us to allow our need for praise to make our best efforts about us and not about God. If we are not humble and our motives aren't genuine, we allow the approval from others create in us an air of arrogance. After seeing Corban's response from all the accolades, I sat him down and read Matthew 5:16 to him. With an inquisitive stare, he asked, "Why does God have to get all of the credit for everything and we don't?" I explained to him that God gets all the glory because if it weren't for Him, we wouldn't be able to do the things we do. God is the one who blesses us with gifts and talents. Therefore, we can say thank you when complimented, but give God the praise too! We can't take God's shine because He is the reason we are shining in the first place. Let's be more like Jesus and give God credit for allowing us to shine before men.

REFLECTIONS

Are you shining your light but taking the opportunity for self-glory or are you giving all the glory to God?

_____

_____

_____

_____

_____

_____

_____

_____

_____

_____

_____

_____

Pearl Thirteen

Say the Name

Then call on me when you are in trouble, and I will
rescue you, and you will give me glory.

Psalm 50:15 (NLT)

There is power in the name of Jesus. It's the strongest and most powerful word we can speak. Jesus' name saves, delivers, redeems, and protects. One Sunday during praise and worship, we sang the song "Say the Name" by Martha Munizi. After singing a few lines of the song, I felt an overwhelming sense of gratefulness sending me into a higher level of worship. It took me back to the time that I understood the depth of this scripture.

I was traveling alone on a familiar highway one morning in October of 2006. The fog made it very difficult to see cars and the road. It was so thick that it felt as if I was driving into the clouds. Suddenly I was facing an 18-wheeler log truck crossing the highway. There was no chance of putting on brakes to avoid the collision. I saw my life flash before my eyes. I didn't have time to pray. I remember screaming Jesus to the top of my lungs when I crashed. For a moment, it was complete silence. When I realized that I was alive, I began to cry out because I was unable to escape my vehicle. The engine of my car was almost sitting in my lap, and my legs were pinned down. I reached for my cell phone and heard someone asking if I was alive. Weeping hysterically, I affirmed that I was. They told me to stay calm that fire and rescue team were on their way.

In Proverbs 18:10 KJV says, "The name of the Lord is a strong tower: the righteous runneth into it and is safe." I am thankful to my Lord and Savior, Jesus Christ for his divine intervention and protection. Not only did He save me from the brink of death, but He allowed me to only come out of the car with a broken ankle and a busted knee. I am blessed to be able to look back on this situation that could have easily taken my life. I knew it was because I called on The Name of Jesus. His power became real to me that day. I know firsthand that He is a life preserver, a savior, and a refuge in life's storms.

Maybe you need healing in your body, mind, spirit, a financial breakthrough, or just need God to do something for you. I assure you that He can, and He will come to your rescue. Often, we underestimate His timeliness because we don't completely trust Him. I encourage you to call on Jesus. I don't know what situation you may be facing right now, but it's nothing He can't handle. If He can allow me to walk away from a mangled vehicle surely, He can rescue you from any situation. Say the Name of Jesus and trust Him not to fall short of His Word.

REFLECTIONS

❖ What difficult situations are you currently facing?

❖ Have you called on the Name of Jesus about that situation?

❖ If not, why? If so, how has your situation changed?

_____

_____

_____

_____

_____

_____

_____

_____

_____

Rashanda Foster

Pearl Fourteen

Damaged Goods

But he said to me, "My grace is sufficient for you, for my power is made perfect in weakness." Therefore I will boast all the more gladly about my weaknesses, so that Christ's power may rest on me.

2 Corinthians 12:9 (NIV)

Have you ever been to the grocery store and noticed items on the shelf that were damaged? I don't know about you, but I often skip over those items or move them out of the way for a can or box with no visible dents. Sometimes, those damaged goods are even taken off the shelf and sold at a discounted price. What's so ironic is like those grocery items, most of us have invisible dents that render us damaged too. When a painful experience hurts us, we often feel useless and worthless. We are often so consumed with our dents that we forget that what's on the inside of us is still good.

For so long I allowed the dents of disappointments, traumatic events, and mistakes to cripple and shape me. I felt that I was damaged to my core. My father's decision not to be an active participant in my life after his divorce from my mother still affects me today. Experiencing sexual assault as a teenager left me feeling confused and I isolated myself. I was unable to connect physically or trust anyone. Being stalked and almost choked to death by a former fiancé affected me in ways I never would've imagined. Giving my heart and love to others at a discount because I didn't know my real value. I kept looking for love in all the wrong places. I could share countless experiences. However, I choose to focus on the fact that in spite of the dents, God's grace is why I am still standing today.

God's grace has allowed me to live with my limitations and weaknesses. Grace has changed the course of my destiny and changed my identity. I was not equipped to face the difficulties of my life on my own. I needed God's help, and I still do. I know today that those experiences were designed to discourage me from using my gifts of speaking and writing to encourage other women. Staying in bondage with my past would've kept me from helping other women. I no longer choose to hide behind my dents.

You may be damaged, but you are useful to God. Everything that was meant to harm you is intended to help you and others. Don't allow your dent to handicap you! God can use damaged goods and produce a beautiful pearl.

REFLECTIONS

What situation has left you feeling damaged?

_____

_____

_____

_____

_____

_____

_____

_____

_____

_____

_____

_____

Pearl Fifteen

Don't Lose Focus

Then I observed that most people are motivated to success because they envy their neighbors. But this, too, is meaningless-like chasing the wind.

Ecclesiastes 4:4 (NLT)

Although this scripture was written 3,000 years ago, it's relevant today more than ever. Social media is good, but it has heightened our potential to envy others after seeing snapshots of their lives leading us to make assumptions about their lifestyles. This leads to competition and making comparisons. We often subconsciously, are motivated by envy and covetousness. Keeping our eyes on people can cause us to lose focus on ourselves and forget our value. Status and titles drive society. It causes many to compare themselves to others instead of rejoicing with them on their successes. Seeing other people with things or in positions that you feel you're more deserving of can lead to envy if you're not careful. An excellent example of envy in the Bible is in I Samuel 18. After hearing a victory song Saul, the King of a nation became envious of his general, David, who had killed more enemies than him. Saul lost sight of his calling and destiny because of his envy for David which resulted in his downfall.

I once ran into a female classmate in a grocery store parking lot in my hometown. She married right out of high school and had two children. She asked me why I was still single. She also said that I should be married with kids by now and not wait until I was too old. I was so offended because I thought to be single and educated with no kids was praise worthy. I let her know that I was happy with my life, wished her well, and went on my way. I didn't realize until much later that our brief conversation made me question who I was. I became discouraged and down on myself because I was looking at friends and people in general who seemed to be getting married and having children. If I can be perfectly honest, for a quick moment I became envious and went into the "God, why them and not me" thinking. I thought because I was thirty years old, trying to live right, college educated, had a good job, financially stable, and a homeowner that I too should be married. I realized that envy is unproductive and it caused undue pain and suffering for me. I got married the first time at the age of 30 with little consultation with God. I threw caution to the wind all because I was listening more to my biological clock and not to God.

For me to attain the things I have seen others achieve, I can't focus on them. I must concentrate on my identity in Christ. I know now that the success of others gives me the opportunity to rejoice with them. God knows what we need in our lives, so we must believe He will give it to us. As women, it's easy to get discouraged when seeing other people happy and in love. His timing isn't in our time, but God is always on time. Draw closer to Him and love Him more than ever before. Use your time as a single woman to prepare your heart and mind for love and marriage. It's not as easy as it looks. I encourage you to trust and believe that God will give you that wedding, job, career, or family that's uniquely yours at His appointed time.

REFLECTIONS

❖ What is distracting you from focusing on God and what He has for you?

❖ How do you plan to eliminate those distractions?

Rashanda Foster

Pearl Sixteen

Highly Favored

Mary asked the angel, "But how can this happen? I am a virgin."

Luke 1: 34

The angel came to Mary to announce the news that not only was she favored by God, but that she would conceive and give birth to Jesus. The angel even told her not to be afraid of the fact that she had found favor with God. Mary was still confused and wanted to know how. Mary felt unqualified and unworthy of such a task because she was just a young girl from a low-income family. What Mary did not realize was that she was blessed and favored by God. God chose (favored) Mary. He chose someone that no one else would have considered to birth His son, Jesus, not because of who she was or what she had done, but because of His grace.

In so many ways I can relate to Mary. I was a little skinny girl from the housing projects. Unlike Mary, I was not without sin or blemish. I had done some things in my life that I was not proud of and that left me feeling unworthy. At 30 years old, God revealed to me that He wanted me to use my experiences to encourage and empower women who were broken. I doubted Him because I did not feel I was worthy or qualified for such a task. I felt like I wasn't that important and no one would want to hear my story. At the age of 35, it was prophesied to me by a total stranger that I was pregnant with a women's ministry and books that would help women. I started writing, but continued to doubt until I received my second prophesy from a total stranger named Prophet Rod, in a Publix parking lot. His prophecy also pertained to me writing books to help women, ministry, and even starting businesses. I finally knew without a doubt what I needed to do for God.

Mary knew that she would be talked about and ostracized for being pregnant out of wedlock. However, she chose to obey God anyway. I could not see past my circumstances enough to realize that God favored me. He went to great lengths to show me His will for my life. I was so busy doubting my fitness for the task because of my past. I was unaware that God saw my past and used it to qualify me. God is not looking for a perfect person. He is looking for a willing person to do His will. Even after giving birth to Jesus, Mary endured difficult times because of the gift she had birthed. Being highly favored does not mean your life will be perfect or that you are exempt from going through hard times. However, like Mary, we are highly favored because God is on our side.

REFLECTIONS

- ❖ What do you believe God is calling you to do?
- ❖ What is keeping you from doing it?
- ❖ How do you plan to begin following God's Will for your life?

_____

_____

_____

_____

_____

_____

_____

_____

_____

_____

Rashanda Foster

Pearl Seventeen

No Hurt Wasted

He comforts us in all our troubles so that we can comfort others. When they are troubled, we will be able to give them the same comfort God has given us.

2 Corinthians 1:4 (NLT)

In this passage, Paul is telling us that God has compassion for us. He is our comforter in all things, and he gives us the strength to comfort others in their time of need by sharing our testimony.

While working as a school counselor, I counseled a student who seemed sad a lot. After some probing, he admitted to me that he was sad because his father wasn't in his life but he sees him all the time in the community. This child could not understand how his father could see him in passing and not want to be in his life. He cried in my arms like a baby over what I call daddy pains. Having been a child and adult who longed for the love of my father, the pain this child felt was far too familiar. At that moment, I began to understand the importance of sharing your hurt to help someone else.

It's difficult to comfort someone when you haven't experienced the level of pain they are experiencing.

The hurt serves a purpose far greater than what we can imagine. Had I not experienced the same type of hurt, I may not have been useful in helping him to heal. I believe that we can neglect the significant value of our hurts by not choosing to heal and grow from them. When we keep our injuries to ourselves and put on a real face like all is well with us, we are wasting an opportunity to share our testimony with someone who shares a similar experience. When we attempt to deal with the hurt on our own, we lose the chance to gain strength available to us from God. Unlike us, God never wastes a hurt. There is always a purpose for it. It's tough to understand that something good can come out of a painful situation. When we admit our hurts and give them to God, we are in a place of total surrender to him. God will comfort us, heal our wounded places, and give us the strength to help others. It doesn't change the fact that the bad experience happened, but it makes me stronger every time I share my experience with someone else.

REFLECTIONS

Will your hurt be wasted? Will you allow God to use your hurt to comfort someone else?

_____

_____

_____

_____

_____

_____

_____

_____

_____

_____

_____

_____

_____

Enduring Trials

*Consider it pure joy, my brothers and sisters, whenever
you face trials of many kinds, because you know that the
testing of your faith produces perseverance. Let
perseverance finish its work so that you may be mature
and complete, not lacking anything.*

James 1:2-4 (NIV)

Not long ago, one of the most difficult things
for me to do was go through difficult times. I
would complain, mope, and whine. The
thought of having joy was inconceivable. I abhorred
hearing my mother say, "Baby, put your big girl
panties on and count it all joy." My attitude during
trials and suffering was that of a spoiled brat. I was only
happy and full of joy when things were going my way.
More than anything, I showed my true colors during
hard times. I was a spiritual wimp.

This scripture above tells us that we should have joy
when we encounter tests and trials. They will provide
an opportunity for growth and stamina. Many people
think happiness and joy are the same, so they find it
difficult to be happy when they are going through
tough times. However, happiness comes from external
things, but joy comes from within. Exuding joy during

our times of testing won't change the circumstances, however, it changes our attitude towards them.

God often allows us to repeat the same test to realize that we should endure it with a different attitude. It seemed as if the longer I complained, the longer the test. I had to understand that tests and trials were a part of God's plan for our lives. Suffering through trials serves a divine purpose. If our goal is to be like Christ, we must experience some pain and suffering. Besides, if we never suffer through anything, we will never mature mentally or spiritually.

Maybe you are being tested at this very moment. Don't be discouraged by what you are going through! It is going to build your spiritual muscle, mature you, and inspire others. You have been assigned this mountain to show others it can be moved. God knows what he is doing! You can still have joy during your trial! Your breakthrough is just around the corner if you keep the right attitude. Go through life with joy and patience just as God instructed us to.

REFLECTIONS

Are you enduring trials with the right attitude?

_____

_____

_____

_____

_____

_____

_____

_____

_____

_____

_____

_____

_____

Pearl Nineteen

Limping but Blessed

"Your name will no longer be Jacob," the man told him. From now on you will be called Israel, because you have fought with God and with men and have won."

Genesis 32:28 (NLT)

This passage is so powerful because it shows how God can change us and our circumstances for the better. Jacob had wronged his brother, Esau, years before God spoke these words to him. Jacob was fearful of Esau coming to attack him. Jacob was determined that he wasn't going to cease praying until God blessed him. During his alone time, he brought his fears before God in prayer and had an encounter with a man. Jacob fought for his blessing even to the point of incurring an injury that could have rendered him helpless. However, Jacob refused to quit fighting until the man blessed him.

Whether Jacob's fight was with his inner man or an angel of God he was transformed and no longer the same after this spiritual encounter. Sometimes, bigger blessings come after we've had to wrestle and fight for something. I choose to believe that God allowed Jacob to have a limp to serve as a reminder of his life changing encounter. Don't allow your limp to distract you from pursuing your blessing. Don't hide your scars; it represents the struggle you survived. Our blessings are coming after God has seen our desire to change, the fight in us, and our determination to receive all that He promised us!

REFLECTIONS

- ❖ Are you facing a battle that it seems you can't win?

- ❖ Will you fight until you are victorious or will you succumb to defeat?

Pearl Twenty

It's Time to be Bold

*If you keep quiet at a time like this, deliverance and relief
for the Jews will arise from some other place, but you and
your relatives will die. Who knows if perhaps you were
made queen for such a time as this?*

Esther 4:14 (NLT)

Esther was chosen to be in a beauty contest
which ultimately led to the King choosing her to
be queen. Esther being favored by King Xerxes
placed her in a position of power. When Queen
Esther's uncle, Mordecai, found out the King's advisor,
Haman had plans to murder all the Jews in the
kingdom, he pleaded with Queen Esther to go to the
King on behalf of the Jews. Despite Esther's position
with the King, by law, no one was to approach him
without being asked to do so. Also, to help the Jews,
Queen Esther would have to reveal to the King that
she too was a Jew, something she had never told
anyone. After being challenged by Mordecai that she
was born for such a time as this, Queen Esther went
boldly before the king to make her request. That
boldness resulted in saving her life and the lives of all
Jewish people in her area.

Many of us were chosen by God to do something to impact the world, and it too will require us to walk in boldness without fear of opposition. My assignment may not be on the level of Queen Esther's, but I was assigned by God to minister to broken women. After having a tearful discussion with my husband, like Queen Esther, I realized I had to admit some issues that I kept from those closest to me. To help other women, I had to first confess that I experienced sexual assault and dealt with the shame and guilt of having an abortion. So many of us suffer in silence and are afraid to tell painful experiences because of our concern for what people will think of us.

I'm learning daily to block out the negative voices and do the will of God wholeheartedly. He wouldn't call me to do something that I wasn't equipped to do. Like Queen Esther, I understand the greater good, and I am willing to risk my reputation for it. When we fully commit our lives to serving God and doing His will, He gives us the boldness we need. There is no time like the present for you to do what others are afraid to.

REFLECTIONS

Will you stand boldly or will you be silent?

_____

_____

_____

_____

_____

_____

_____

_____

_____

_____

_____

_____

Pearl Twenty-One

No, not yet!

The Lord is near to the brokenhearted and saves the crushed in spirit.

Psalm 34:18 (NLT)

This scripture is encouraging because not only does it warn us of disappointment, but that the Lord is always there for us. Some people have experienced so much frustration that they have let it define them. We can't allow disappointment to determine who we are and how we navigate through life. You lost your job, you did not get that job you wanted, you were overlooked, you trusted someone with your heart, and they hurt you. IT happened, now what? IT may have happened, but it does not make you any less of a person or determine your destiny.

While in school for my second Master's in School Counseling, I decided I wanted to work with the education system, so I began applying for jobs. I recall interviewing for a counselor position at a middle school in my hometown. The interview went great! I was told by the principal that I had the job. A week passed, and I found out the job was given to a relative of someone on the school board. I was plagued with negative thoughts about that school system because of the way my situation was handled. For a short time, that silent "No" caused me to question if I would ever be a school counselor. I began to focus on my studies. A month later, I received a call from a friend whose husband was a principal and needed a counselor. When I answered the phone, she said, "Rashanda, do you want a school counseling job?" I immediately said, "Yes, but I am pregnant and due in three months. I hope that won't be a problem." I went for the interview the next day and was hired to be the school counselor. I grew from that experience and realized that God said, "No, not yet." He had something else in store for me, and I would receive it in His time, not mine.

Disappointment comes when we want something bad! Hearing a no can be crushing and painful. It is natural to cry and be frustrated. However, you cannot allow disappointment to linger in your heart and mind too long and cause you to become bitter. Take the time to verbally express your disappointment because holding it in can be a hindrance later. Look at that no as a delay, not a denial. There is power in no. It can propel or stagnate. Allow that disappointment to move you to a place of self-discovery and personal development. Grow from that no. Do not go through life living in defeat and afraid to try again for fear of disappointment! We must accept the fact that things won't always go as planned. Allow disappointment to strengthen you by yielding your will to God and increasing your faith in God. We often experience disappointment when we have gotten out of God's will for our lives. That is not to say we won't experience disappointment when He is leading us, but we can be assured that He has our best interest at heart.

Jeremiah 29:11 NLT says, "For I know the plans I have for you," says the Lord. "They are plans for good and not for disaster, to give you a future and hope." Disappointment can very well be a part of God's plan. I encourage you to pray and ask God to show you what He wants you to gain from disappointment. You cannot quit. Keep moving forward!

REFLECTIONS

❖ List a few disappointments you've had to endure.

❖ Have you allowed those disappointments to alter your life or plans?

_____

_____

_____

_____

_____

_____

_____

_____

_____

_____

_____

Rashanda Foster

I'm Salty

You are the salt of the earth. But what good is salt if it has lost its flavor? Can you make it salty again? It will be thrown out and trampled underfoot as worthless.

Matthew 5:13 (NLT)

In this scripture, Jesus was talking to his followers. He likened believers to salt. Now salt is a mineral used to add flavor and to preserve. Jesus used salt to illustrate how Christians are needed to bring balance and substance to a dying world. He also asked them, "What good is salt if it has lost its flavor?" In other words, what's the point of calling yourself a Christian but you're not doing anything to impact the lives of others in this world. If you are not showing the love of Christ to those who don't look or believe like you, you are not the salt.

If you watch one minute of the news, you'll see that there is so much evil in this world. It is evident that there is a lack of moral compass because the "anything goes" mentality has become standard in the world. People are no longer friendly and loving. Something is missing, and Christians are that something. Many times, we don't show the love of God to people outside of our family, church, or circle and that's where it's needed the most.

Do you know how precious and valuable you are to this world and the Kingdom of God? Woman of God, you cannot allow your past experiences or present circumstances cause you to lose you the flavor. When you are salty, you don't hesitate to help that random person who is having car trouble on the side of the road; you don't mind giving money to someone who is homeless when they ask, and speak kind words to that cashier that is rude to you. This bland world needs sprinkles of salt in abundance. Don't be content with staying in the salt shaker! Saying you are the salt is not enough. The only way salt can be useful is if you use it for the purpose it was designed.

REFLECTIONS

Are you salty or has life caused you to lose your flavor?

_____

_____

_____

_____

_____

_____

_____

_____

_____

_____

_____

_____

_____

_____

Pearl Twenty-Three

Count the Costs

For the wages of sin is death, but the free gift of God is eternal life through Christ Jesus our Lord.

Romans 6:23 (NLT)

I heard "count the cost" so many times from my mother as a young adult when I was contemplating doing something, in the middle of something, or if she thought I was about to do something. It was her way of warning me to consider the consequences before I acted. This warning often fell on deaf ears when I had my mind set on doing what I wanted to do. "Count the Cost" was just a cliché until I found myself in sticky situations suffering from self-inflicted wounds.

I came to understand this scripture all too well. God paid a high price for us by allowing His son Jesus to suffer unfair treatment, brutal death, and burial to cover our sins. Because of the enormous sacrifice God made on our behalf, our lives, actions, and decisions should reflect our appreciation. The high price He paid for our sins is not a license for us to live and do as we please. We must understand that it is not the will of God for us to live in sin. We pay with our joy, peace, self-esteem, happiness, finances, and sometimes our children reap the consequences of our actions.

There is nothing more depressing than living life below your God-given potential because we chose sin over righteousness. We know the right way, but we choose the wrong way. When you opt to participate in activities that God's Word deems sinful, some consequences come at a cost you could never afford.

God loves and cares for you, and that is why He gave us the warning in Romans 6:23. Just as we receive warnings about weather, there are costs associated if we don't take heed to the warnings that could cost us eternal life.

Maybe you are living a life that's contrary to the Word of God. Momentary pleasure is not worth the guilt, shame, and other consequences that will occur. Living a life of sin is not God's will for your life. God already paid the ultimate price for you and me. Don't serve a life sentence by staying in a bad situation! Repent and be forgiven!

REFLECTIONS

Are you honoring God's sacrifice with your life?

More Than Enough

Who can find a virtuous and capable wife? She is more precious than rubies.

Proverbs 31:10 (NLT)

If you are like me when you read all of Proverbs 31 you are either encouraged or intimidated. I say that because the characteristics of a Godly woman are listed and when I compare myself and the woman described, I fall short. However, God established the value of a Godly woman early before listing the things she does. He says she is worth more than expensive gems. To God, she is not just enough she is more than sufficient.

I once dated someone that never wanted to put a title on our relationship. To me, we were exclusive, and I treated our relationship as such. However, I found out that he was seeing other women. I was hurt badly. I was so blinded by my feelings for him that I neglected my value and what I deserved.

We often need to be reminded of how valuable we are to God when situations and people in our lives cause us to question our value. I have experienced relationships and situations that almost depleted my self-esteem and self-worth. As women, when we experience being cheated on, rejection from a parent, or a failed relationship, we automatically think and feel as if something is wrong with us. We would believe things like if only I were prettier, smarter, or more attractive then maybe they would want me.

Woman of God, no matter how bad you have been hurt, know that you are precious and valuable to God. You don't have to accept less than you deserve by discounting your morals and standards. God has already established your worth, and that's more than enough. You are beautifully and wonderfully made. A person who knows your worth will treat you as the precious gem that you are.

REFLECTIONS

Has the treatment of others caused you to discount your worth?

_____

_____

_____

_____

_____

_____

_____

_____

_____

_____

_____

_____

I Have Confidence

So do not throw away this confident trust in the Lord. Remember the great reward it brings you! Patient endurance is what you need now, so that you will continue to do God's will. Then you will receive all that he has promised.

Hebrews 10: 35-36 (NLT)

The writer of Hebrews encouraged Christians who were being persecuted because of their faith, to continue in the Christian faith and that they will be rewarded by God. We may not have experienced persecution of this magnitude, but we all will and have faced trials. Therefore, we are still encouraged by these verses to have enduring faith in times of trials.

Have you ever been in an awkward situation and felt like it was going to get the best of you? I have, and the only thing that I had to rely on was my faith in God. I recalled the times before when I felt the very same way, and he brought me through that situation. I know that if he did it for me that time, he would do it for me this time if I keep the faith. My confidence does not come from just reading His word, but by believing it and seeing it.

We don't know true trust in God until our faith is tested. Tests and obstacles are sure to come. So, when sickness knocks on your front door, an unexpected bill appears in your mailbox, your children begin to rebel, or tragedy strikes, don't throw away your confidence in God! Keep trusting God to see you through. Put your mind in rewind and recall what he did for you before! Don't you dare give in to the pressure and the stress! A confident woman of God perseveres knowing that God will not fall short of his promises.

REFLECTIONS

Do you keep your confidence in God when trials come?

_____

_____

_____

_____

_____

_____

_____

_____

_____

_____

_____

_____

_____

Pearl Twenty-Six
The Real MVP

Her children arise and call her blessed; her husband also, and praises her.

Proverbs 31:28 (NIV)

If you ask most mothers if they feel appreciated they would probably say no. Most children do not grow to appreciate their mothers until they are in their 20's and some even in their 30's. I remember getting emotional after seeing NBA Player, Kevin Durant, acknowledge his mother during his MVP acceptance speech as "The Real MVP" because of all her love, sacrifice, and support for him. His appreciation for his mother is what every mother hopes to hear. It was not until I was in college that I became acutely aware of the magnitude of my mother's influence on my life. A Godly mother is the source of wisdom, love, sacrifice, and patience for her children.

I was in the third grade when my parents divorced, leaving my mother to be a single mom. For years, I watched her be a super mom to my brother and me. From her only eating one meal a day so that we would have enough to eat, paying rent for both of us with help from my grandparents for our apartments in college, and to purchasing a car for us to share though she did not have one of her own. Thinking of her sacrifices brings me to tears. Although she hardly ever verbalized her frustration or difficulties, I know she had some. I know it was only because of her relationship with the Lord that she could endure the difficult times without us seeing the stress and strain. I glean Godly wisdom and kindness from my mother even more now that I am a wife and a mother. The strength and faith in God I have seen with my mother over the years has been my driving force and biggest blessing.

Maybe you are a single mother or mother who feels unappreciated. Don't be discouraged. I encourage you to keep doing what you are doing! The strength you show, lessons you teach, trials you endure, daily prayers, tears you cry, and sacrifices you make are not in vain. Your life and your experiences are of great value to your children. They too will arise and call you blessed!

REFLECTIONS

❖ Have you become discouraged because your sacrifices are not being acknowledged?

❖ When did you appreciate the sacrifices of your mother?

_____

_____

_____

_____

_____

_____

_____

_____

_____

_____

Pearl Twenty-Seven
Where Is Your Faith

And he said to her, "Daughter, your faith has made you well. Go in peace. Your suffering is over."

Mark 5:34 (NLT)

This story is about a woman with an issue of blood who was desperate to be healed. She pressed her way through a crowd, touched the hem of Jesus' robe, and received her healing. She received her healing because of her faith in Jesus. After twelve long years, she had gone broke going to doctor after doctor to no avail. I wonder, where was her faith in Jesus during those twelve years?

If you examine all the miracles in the Bible, it took each person seeking healing or deliverance having faith to receive what it is they needed from Jesus. The woman had heard all about the miracles that Jesus performed, and she grew an enormous faith just from hearing people talk about him. I believe the woman didn't have a name before her touch of faith because her issue had become who she was instead of what she had. Jesus called her Daughter after he healed her sickness. He does that same thing for us when we seek Him out of desperation and faith to heal us of our issues.

How many times have you heard the incredible miracles that Jesus has done for people you know but you don't have faith in him for your issues? Like the woman, we often seek to heal our issues from everyone else and making Jesus our last resort. However, it's so good to know that he doesn't hold that against us. We should mirror this woman's faith when we suffer with our own issues. She had the courage and faith to approach Jesus for what she needed. With her faith and a touch, she received her healing. If you believe in faith, you can also hear, "Daughter your faith has made you well. Go in peace. Your suffering is over."

REFLECTIONS

What are you waiting on for your deliverance? Where is your faith in God?

_____

_____

_____

_____

_____

_____

_____

_____

_____

_____

_____

_____

_____

Stay Lit

The light shines in the darkness, and the darkness can never extinguish it.

John 1:5 (NLT)

This scripture is so important. It encourages us to be the light, and it acknowledges darkness as an adversary and a struggle. Light exemplifies life with Jesus and darkness is life without Jesus. However, it tells us despite the struggle, be the light of Jesus, the light of the world, and the light that shines in the dark.

Think about when there is a storm, and the lights go out. We automatically search for a flashlight or candle so that we can navigate through the darkness. We should be that candle or flashlight illuminating Jesus when storms of life come and darkness tries to take over. I will go a step further and say be that light when people are trying to attack your character. Be that light when someone has hurt or offended you. The enemy despises light, and that is why Jesus was crucified.

A few weeks ago, my family and I went to a restaurant for breakfast. Our waitress came to the table with a very nonchalant attitude and seemed preoccupied. To add insult to injury, we watched people who were seated after us get their food while we were still waiting. When our orders finally arrived, they were wrong. We were a bit irritated with our waitress and felt we were being treated differently because of our race. Instead of getting out of character like my two sons wanted to do, we kindly reordered our food. When it was time to pay, my husband, and I discussed that we would not skip out on the tip, but we would tip far above what she deserved. What happened next was amazing! On our way out of the restaurant, that same waitress ran up to my husband and me. She thanked us, apologized for the terrible service, and hugged me. I simply told her that I had no idea what she was going through, but I hope God blesses her. In this situation, I could have easily acted out like the women we see on Basketball Wives or Housewives of Atlanta, but I chose to shine anyway. She experienced the love of Jesus even though she had not given us the service we deserved. My light exposed the darkness in her, and her darkness didn't extinguish my light.

Throughout your lives, you will be faced with darkness, but be determined to stay lit. When you shine your light, you show the love and character of Jesus. It could be as simple as giving a helping hand to a total stranger or as difficult as being nice to someone who does not like you. Despite the darkness, shine anyway!

REFLECTIONS

❖ Are you succumbing to the darkness or being a light?

❖ How can you be a light in your daily life?

Rashanda Foster

_____

_____

_____

_____

_____

_____

_____

_____

_____

_____

_____

_____

_____

_____

_____

Lose to Win

*Then Jesus said to his disciples, "If any of you wants to
be my follower you must give up your own way, take up
your cross, and follow me. If you try to hang on to your
life, you will lose it. But if you give up your life for my sake,
you will save it.*

Matthew 16:24-25 (NLT)

J esus tells us in these scriptures that if we proclaim
or want to be a Christian, we have to say no to
the things we want and place his will and desires
over our own. While this may seem complicated and
rather intimidating, it is necessary.

Are we willing to give up our selfish desires to be a
follower of Jesus? We must surrender our need to
control every situation and deny ourselves the things
that please us, but don't glorify Jesus. Yes, single
woman, that means not sleeping with that man
because you want a warm body in your bed. It also
means not being in a relationship with someone with
whom you are unequally yoked. Woman of God, that
means putting your husband's needs before your own
and submitting to him. It means speaking up for
righteousness to the unrighteous, no matter how
uncomfortable it may be. It means giving your money,

time, and talents to God first instead of giving Him sloppy seconds. To do what Jesus said in this scripture requires losing or giving up some things. I think the church today is looking a lot like the world because people are not willing to abandon their own selfish desires to follow Christ effectively.

Fantasia has a song," Lose to Win." She talked about letting go of an unhealthy relationship with a man who was using her, taking her for granted, and making herself available for a better man who would treat her better. I was one of those women who loved this song, and I'm sure you were too. What she said in the song was much like what Jesus said in the scripture above. To save our lives, we have to lose or give up those things we want to win what we need. Perhaps some things in your life are hindering you from fully following Jesus Christ. Whether it is a man, a woman, habit, or lifestyle, you must decide to live God's way.

REFLECTIONS

What are you willing to lose or give up, to win with Jesus?

_____

_____

_____

_____

_____

_____

_____

_____

_____

_____

_____

_____

_____

Pearl Thirty

Beauty for Ashes

*To all who mourn in Israel, he will give a crown of beauty
for ashes, a joyous blessing instead of mourning, festive
praise instead of despair. In their righteousness, they will
be like great oaks that the Lord has planted for his own
glory.*

Isaiah 61:3 (NLT)

If you have a fireplace, I'm sure you enjoy the beauty
of the fire from the burning of the wood, but dread
the tedious task of cleaning and disposing the
ashes. I didn't realize, until some years ago, that those
ashes can be used to do so many things like polish
silverware, gardening, or planting to add nutrients to
the soil.

Just like wood that was burned and became ashes,
negative experiences in our lives have the same effect.
Indeed, we are changed by negative experiences, but
God gives us beauty for the ashes. He uses those
ashes for His glory. After I had suffered from all the
negative experiences that were meant to destroy me,
God gave me a voice to help those who did not have
one. Instead of focusing on the things that happened,
God wiped away my tears and replaced my sadness
with joy that only He can give. Like ashes, I am using

my experiences to polish and add nutrients to women who need help to grow from their experiences.

Maybe you had a negative experience that was intended by Satan to destroy you. You are not what happened to you. Don't you dare give in to despair! God will give you beauty for your ashes. He will wipe your tears and restore your joy. The ashes left after that experience are what make you beautiful. Your ashes serve a purpose. You are the righteousness that God will plant for His glory.

REFLECTIONS

Do you see the beauty in your negative experiences?

_____

_____

_____

_____

_____

_____

_____

_____

_____

_____

_____

_____

_____

_____

_____

_____

_____

_____

_____

_____

_____

_____

_____

_____

_____

_____

_____

_____

Pearl Thirty-One

Pretty Peculiar

But ye are a chosen generation, a royal priesthood, an holy nation, a peculiar people; that ye should shew forth the praises of him who hath called you out of darkness into his marvelous light:

I Peter 2:9 (KJV)

In a world where individuality is almost nonexistent, this verse is confirmation that we should stand out instead of fitting in once we have accepted Christ into our lives. God is our leading authority. If He says we are chosen, royalty, and peculiar, we must believe what He says.

Society has a way of influencing our thoughts about what is acceptable, who we should be, and what we should look like. However, God says that we are accepted (chosen), we belong to Him, we are royal, holy, unique and unlike any other people in this world. We are not what happened to us, we are not who others say we are, we are who God says we are.

Maybe if we believed what God says about us, we would live accordingly. As people of God, we should live differently than those without Christ in their lives. Women of God don't have to dress provocatively to get attention from men. A man of God will notice her because she stands out from the rest. Unlike other women, a woman of God carries herself in a way that others will know she is connected to God when they interact with her.

It is normal for you to be different than other women. You do not have to change who you are to fit in. God says that you are His chosen, so you do not have to be concerned about acceptance from anyone else.

REFLECTIONS

What makes you peculiar? How do you stand out from the crowd?

_____

_____

_____

_____

_____

_____

_____

_____

_____

_____

_____

_____

Final Words from the Author

It's no accident you chose to read this devotional. For every woman who took the time to purchase and read this devotional, I am thankful for you. I encourage you to allow Pearls of Grace to be a catalyst for your healing and a source that ignites a fire in you to adequately address the pains of your past. I know uncovering issues that you have buried deep within is not easy. However, you cannot heal what hasn't been uncovered. Now dig deep, gather your pearls, and wear them proudly. Your pearls signify that you made it through the toughest times, but by God's grace, you survived. It is my hope that you will share your pearls with another woman who may not understand the value of hers. Please know that I am praying that God will give you the strength and courage you need so that you too can use your story for His glory.

Stay Connected

Thank you for purchasing Pearls of Grace. Rashanda would like to connect with you! Below are a few ways you can stay connected to Rashanda.

FACEBOOK Rashanda N. Foster
INSTAGRAM Rashanda N. Foster
WEBSITE www.rashandafoster.com
EMAIL info@rashandafoster.com

Made in the USA
Las Vegas, NV
18 November 2022

59731569R00085